how to

how to cure

a fanatic

AMOS OZ

princeton university press

princeton and oxford

The two essays were originally published in Great Britain in 2004 by Vintage. These essays were originally delivered as speeches in Germany in 2002. They have been edited here for the English-language edition.

Requests for permission to reproduce material from this work should be sent to Permissions, Princeton University Press

Published by Princeton University Press, 41 William Street, Princeton, New Jersey 08540
press.princeton.edu

Fourth printing, and first paperback printing, 2010
Paperback ISBN: 978-0-691-14863-2

The Library of Congress has cataloged the cloth edition of this book as follows

Oz, Amos.
How to cure a fanatic / Amos Oz.
  p.   cm.
Previously published, without interview, as: Help us to divorce. Includes the essay Between right and right and an interview of Amos Oz conducted by Brigitta van Rheinberg.

ISBN-13: 978-0-691-12669-2 (cloth : alk. paper)
ISBN-10: 0-691-12669-0 (cloth : alk. paper)

1. Arab-Israeli conflict,—1993–.   2. Fanaticism—Palestine.
3. Land tenure—Palestine.   4. Oz, Amos—Interviews.
5. Authors, Israeli—Interviews.   I. Rheinberg, Brigitta van.
II. Oz, Amos. Between right and right.   III. Oz, Amos. Help us to divorce.   IV. Title.
DS119.76 .O93   2006
956.05/3—dc22   2005056559

This book has been composed in ITC New Baskerville

Printed on acid-free paper. ∞

Printed in the United States of America

10 9 8 7 6 5

contents

vii   *Foreword by*
       Nadine Gordimer

1   Between Right and Right

37   How to Cure a Fanatic

73   The Order of the Teaspoon:
       An Interview with Amos Oz

foreword by
Nadine Gordimer

Amos Oz is the voice of sanity coming out of confusion, the lying, hysterical babble of world rhetoric about current conflicts. In the brilliant clarity of "How to Cure a Fanatic," he analyzes the twisted historical roots that produce the evil flower of violence, seeded again and again. He brings us to face the nature of fanaticism, its evolution. He doesn't offer a cure-all.

But he convinces irrefutably that the Israeli-Palestinian conflict is "Not a religious war, not a war of cultures, not a disagreement between two traditions, but simply a real-estate dispute

over whose house this is." And he is not afraid
to stake his vision and politico-moral integrity
in the belief that the dispute can be resolved.
"Between Right and Right" is a down-to-ground
solution for which he advocates the necessity
of imagination in what human beings in certain situations basically need in order to begin
to define and respect each other's space. The
ironic humor with which he illuminates the
vitally serious makes it all the more telling.

between right and right

between right and right

Who are the good guys? That's what every well-meaning European, left-wing European, intellectual European, liberal European always wants to know, first and foremost. Who are the good guys in the film and who are the bad guys. In this respect Vietnam was easy: The Vietnamese people were the victims, and the Americans were the bad guys. The same with apartheid: You could easily see that apartheid was a crime and that the struggle for civil rights, for liberation and equality, and for human dignity was right. The struggle between colonialism and imperialism, on the one hand, and the victims of colonialism and imperialism, on the other, seems relatively simple—you can tell the good guys from the bad. When it comes to the foundations of the Israeli-Arab conflict, in particular the Israeli-Palestinian conflict, things are not so straight-forward. And I am afraid I am not going to make things any easier for you by saying simply: These are the angels, these are the devils; you just have to support the angels, and good will prevail over evil. The Israeli-Palestinian conflict is not a Wild West movie. It is not a struggle between good and evil, rather it is a tragedy in the ancient and most precise sense of the word: a clash between right and right, a clash between one very powerful, deep, and convincing claim, and another very different but no less convincing, no less powerful, no less humane claim.

The Palestinians are in Palestine because Palestine is the homeland, and the only home-land, of the Palestinian people. In the same way in which Holland is the homeland of the Dutch, or Sweden the homeland of the Swedes. The Israeli Jews are in Israel because there is no other country in the world that the Jews, as a people, as a nation, could ever call home. As individuals, yes, but not as a people, not as a nation. The Palestinians have tried, unwillingly, to live in other Arab countries. They were rejected, sometimes even humiliated and persecuted by the so-called Arab family. They were made aware in the most painful way of their "Palestinianness"; they were not wanted by Lebanese or Syrians, by Egyptians or Iraqis. They had to learn the hard way that they are Palestinians, and that's the only country that they can hold on to. In a strange way the Jewish people and the Palestinian people have had a somewhat parallel historical experience. The Jews were kicked out of Europe; my parents were kicked out of Europe some seventy years ago. Just like the

Palestinians were first kicked out of Palestine
and then out of the Arab countries, or almost.
When my father was a little boy in Poland, the
streets of Europe were covered with graffiti,
"Jews, go back to Palestine," or sometimes
worse: "Dirty Yids, piss off to Palestine." When
my father revisited Europe fifty years later, the
walls were covered with new graffiti, "Jews, get
out of Palestine."

People in Europe keep sending me wonderful invitations to spend a rosy weekend in
a delightful resort with Palestinian partners,
Palestinian colleagues, Palestinian counter-
parts, so that we can learn to know one another, to like one another, to drink a cup of
coffee together, so that we realize that no one
has horns and tails—and the trouble will go
away. This is based on the widespread sentimental European idea that every conflict is
essentially no more than a misunderstanding. A little group therapy, a touch of family

counseling, and everyone will live happily ever after. Well, first, I have bad news for you: Some conflicts are very real; they are much worse than a mere misunderstanding. And then I have some sensational news for you: There is no essential misunderstanding between Palestinian Arab and Israeli Jew. The Palestinians want the land they call Palestine. They have very strong reasons to want it. The Israeli Jews want exactly the same land for exactly the same reasons, which provides for a perfect understanding between the parties, and for a terrible tragedy. Rivers of coffee drunk together cannot extinguish the tragedy of two peoples claiming, and I think rightly claiming, the same small country as their one and only national homeland in the whole world. So, drinking coffee together is wonderful and I'm all for it, especially if it is Arabic coffee, which is infinitely better than Israeli coffee. But drinking coffee cannot do away with the trouble.

What we need is not just coffee and a better understanding. What we need is a painful compromise. The word "compromise" has a terrible reputation in Europe. Especially among young idealists who always regard compromise as opportunism, as something dishonest, as something sneaky and shady, as a mark of a lack of integrity. Not in my vocabulary. For me the word "compromise" means life. And the opposite of compromise is not idealism, not devolution; the opposite of compromise is fanaticism and death. We need to compromise. Compromise, not capitulation. A compromise means that the Palestinian people should never go down on their knees; neither should the Israeli Jewish people.

I'm going to discuss the nature of such a compromise, but right at the outset I should tell you that this compromise will be very painful—because both peoples love the country and both peoples, Israeli Jews and Palestinian Arabs, have equally deep, though different historical and emotional roots in the country. One of the components of this tragedy, one of the aspects that has a certain irony about it, is the fact that many Israeli Jews don't recognize how deep is the Palestinian emotional connection to the land. And many Palestinians fail to recognize just how deep is the Jewish connection to the same land. And this recognition comes in a painful way and as a painful process for both nations. It is a route paved with shattered dreams and broken illusions and injured hopes and blown-up slogans from the past on both sides.

I have worked for many years for the Israeli Peace Now movement. In fact, I worked for an Israeli-Palestinian peace long before Peace Now was established in 1978. Back in 1967, immediately after the Six Day War, I was among the very first and very few Israeli Jews who immediately advocated the idea of negotiating the future of the West Bank and Gaza not with Jordan or Egypt but with the Palestinian leadership and yes, with the PLO, who at that time refused even to pronounce the word "Israel." It was a strange experience in those days. And at that moment, the Israeli peace movement was injured.

But let's be very clear that the Israeli peace movement has not been a twin sister of the pacifist movements in Europe, or in America, during the years of the Vietnam War or more recently. We are not of the idea that if Israel pulls out of the occupied territories, everything will be solved overnight. Nor are we of the simplistic idea that Israel is the bad guy, certainly not the only bad guy in this story. We are pro-peace, but not necessarily pro-Palestine. We are very critical of the Palestinian leadership. I personally am as critical of the Palestinian leadership as I am of the Israeli leadership. And I will come to that later. But the argument between ourselves and some European peace movements cuts deeper. I have been personally on the battlefield twice in my life, for the first time as a reservist soldier with a tank unit on the Egyptian front in Sinai in 1967 and again on the Syrian front in the 1973 war. It was the most horrible experience of my life, and yet I'm not ashamed that I fought in those two wars. I'm not a pacifist in the sentimental sense of the word. If once again I felt that there was a real danger of my country being completely wiped off the map and my people butchered, I would fight again, although I'm an old man. But I would only fight if I thought it was a matter of life and death, or if I thought anybody was trying to turn me or the next person into a slave. I would never fight—I would prefer to go to jail—over extra territories. I would never fight for an extra bedroom for the nation. I would never fight over holy places or holy sites. I

would never fight over so-called national interests. But I would fight, and fight like the
devil, for life and for freedom and for nothing else.

Now this may create a certain gap between
myself and the regular European pacifist, who
maintains that the ultimate evil in the world is
war. In my vocabulary war is terrible, yet the
ultimate evil is not war but aggression. If in
1939 the whole world except for Germany
had maintained that war was the worst of all
evils in the world, then Hitler would have
been lord of the universe by now. So, when
you recognize aggression, you have to fight
against it, wherever it comes from. But only
over life and freedom, not extra territory or
extra resources.

When I coined the phrase "Make Peace Not
Love," I was not, of course, preaching against
making love. But I was, to some extent, trying to
remove the widespread sentimental mishmash

of peace and love and brotherhood and compassion and forgiveness and concession and so on, which makes people think that if only people would drop their weapons, the world would immediately become a marvelous, loving place. Personally, I happen to believe that love is a rare commodity. I think that a human being, at least in my experience, can love ten people. If he's very generous he can love twenty people. If he's exceedingly lucky, he may be loved by twenty people. If someone says to me that she loves Latin America, or he loves the Third World, it is too superficial to be meaningful. As a popular song lamented many years ago, "There's just not enough love to go 'round." I don't think love is the virtue by which we solve international problems. We need other virtues. We need a sense of justice, but we also need common sense; we need imagination, a deep ability to imagine the other, sometimes to put ourselves in the skin of the other. We need the rational ability to compromise and sometimes to make sacrifices and concessions, but we don't need to commit suicide for the sake of peace, "I'll kill myself so that you will be happy." Or, "I want you to kill yourself because that will make me happy." And those two attitudes are not dissimilar; they are closer than you think.

In my view, the opposite of war is not love, and the opposite of war is not compassion, and the opposite of war is not generosity or brotherhood, or forgiveness. No, the opposite of war is peace. Nations need to live in peace. If I see in my lifetime the State of Israel and the State of Palestine, living next door to each other as decent neighbors without oppression, without exploitation, without bloodshed, without terror, without violence, I will be satisfied even if love does not prevail. And, as the poet Robert Frost reminds us, "Good fences make good neighbors."

One of the things that makes this conflict particularly hard is the fact that the Israeli-Palestinian, the Israeli-Arab conflict, is essentially a conflict between two victims. Two victims of the same oppressor. Europe—which colonized the Arab world, exploited it, humiliated it, trampled upon its culture, controlled it and used it as an imperialistic playground—is the same Europe that discriminated against the Jews, persecuted them, harassed them, and finally, mass-murdered them in an unprecedented crime of genocide. Now, you would think that two victims would immediately develop between themselves a sense of solidarity—as, for instance, in the poetry of Bertolt Brecht. But in real life, some of the worst conflicts are precisely the conflicts between two victims of the same oppressor. Two children of the same cruel parent do not necessarily love each other. Very often they see in each other the exact image of the cruel parent.

And this is precisely the case not just between Israeli and Palestinian but between Jew and Arab. Each of the parties looks at the other and sees the image of their past oppressors. In contemporary Arabic literature, though not in all of it (and I have to make a reservation here; I can read Arabic literature only in translation), the Jew, especially the Israeli Jew, is often pictured as an extension of the white, sophisticated, tyrannizing, colonizing, cruel, heartless Europe of the past. They are depicted as the colonialists who came to the Middle East once again, this time disguised as Zionists, to tyrannize, to colonize, and to exploit. Very often Arabs, even some sensitive Arab writers, fail to see us as what we, Israeli Jews, really are—a bunch of half-hysterical refugees and survivors, haunted by dreadful nightmares, traumatized not only by Europe but also by the way we were treated in Arabic and Islamic countries. Half the population of Israel consists of people who were kicked out of Arabic and Islamic countries. Israel is indeed one large Jewish refugee camp. Though half of us are actually Jewish refugees from Arab countries, Arabs don't see us this way; they see us as an extension of colonialism. By the same token we Israeli Jews don't see the Arabs, particularly the Palestinians, as what they are: victims of centuries of oppression, exploitation, colonialism, and humiliation. No, we see them as pogrom-makers and Nazis who wrapped themselves in kaffiyehs and grew mustaches and got suntanned, but are in the same old game of cutting the throats of Jews for fun. In short, they are our past oppressors all over again. In this respect there is a deep ignorance on both sides: not ignorance about the political purposes and the goals, but about the backgrounds, about the deep traumas of the two victims.

I've been very critical of the Palestinian

national movement for many years. Some of the reasons are historical, some are not. Mostly I have been critical of the Palestinian national movement for failing to realize how genuine the Jewish connection to the land of Israel is. Failing to realize that modern Israel is not a product of a colonialist enterprise, or at least failing to tell it to their people. I should tell you immediately that I'm equally critical of generations of Israeli Zionists, who failed to imagine that there is a Palestinian people, a real people with actual and legitimate rights. So both leaderships past and, yes, present are guilty of either not understanding the tragedy, or not telling their people.

Well, I don't believe in a sudden burst of mutual love between Israel and Palestine. I don't expect that once some miraculous formula is found the two antagonists will suddenly hug each other in tears in a Dostoyevskian scene of long-lost brothers reconciled—"O my brother, will you ever forgive me, how could I be so terrible, take the land, who cares about the land, just give me your love." Unfortunately, I don't expect anything like this. I don't expect a honeymoon either. If anything, I expect a fair and just divorce between Israel and Palestine. And divorces are never happy, even when they are more or less just. They still hurt, they are painful. Especially this particular divorce, which is going to be a very peculiar divorce, because the two divorcing parents are definitely staying in the same apartment. No one is moving out. And the apartment being very small, it will be necessary to decide who gets bedroom A and who gets bedroom B and how about the living room; and the apartment being so small, some special arrangement has to be made about the bathroom and the kitchen. Very inconvenient. But better than the kind of living hell that everyone is going through now in this beloved country. A country where

Palestinian men, women, and children are daily oppressed, haunted, humiliated, deprived by the cruel Israeli military government. A country where Israeli people are daily terrorized by ruthless indiscriminate terrorist attacks on civilians, men, women, children, schoolboys, teenagers, shoppers in a mall. Anything is preferable to this! Especially, a fair divorce. And eventually perhaps, after we have conducted this painful and fair divorce by creating two states, divided roughly according to demographic realities—and I'm not going to try to draw the map here, but I can tell you, in a nutshell, that essentially the lines should be similar to the pre-1967 lines, with some mutually agreed-upon modifications and some special arrangements for the disputed holy places in Jerusalem—once this divorce is conducted and partition is created, I believe Israelis and Palestinians will be quick to hop over the partition for a cup of coffee together.

That will be the time for coffee together. Moreover, I predict that shortly after the partition solution is implemented, we shall be in the position to cook our meals together in the little kitchen, by which I mean develop a shared economy. Perhaps a common Middle East market. Perhaps a Middle East currency. Of one thing I can assure Europeans: Our conflict in the Middle East is indeed painful and bloody and cruel and stupid, but it's not going to take us a thousand years to produce our equivalent of the Euro currency of the Middle East. We will be faster than you were, and shed less blood that you did. So, before you people look down on us—Jewish idiots, Arab idiots, cruel people, fanatical people, extremist people, violent people—be a little more careful wagging your fingers at all of us. Our bloody history is going to be shorter than your bloody history. I know it's very dangerous to make prophecies when you come from my part of the world. There is a lot of competition in the prophecy business over here. But I can stick my neck out and predict that we are not going to spend hundreds of years butchering one another in the time-honored European tradition. We will be quicker than that. How much quicker? I wish I could answer you. I never underestimate the shortsightedness and stupidity of political leadership on both sides. But it will happen.

Moreover, the crucial first step ought to be, must be, a two-state solution. Israel must go back to what has been the initial Israeli proposition since 1948 and even before, from the beginning: recognition for recognition, statehood for statehood, independence for independence, security for security. Neighborliness for neighborliness, respect for respect. The Palestinian leadership for its part must turn to its own people and say at last, loud and clear, something that it has never succeeded in pronouncing, namely that Israel is not an accident of history, that Israel is not an intrusion, that Israel happens to be the homeland of the Israeli Jews—no matter how painful this is for the Palestinians. Just as we Israeli Jews have to say loud and clear that Palestine is the homeland of the Palestinian people, inconvenient as this may seem to us.

The worst part of the Israeli-Arab, the Israeli-Palestinian conflict, is not now, it's in those many years, many decades when the two parties could not even pronounce each other's name. When the Palestinians and other Arabs had a real difficulty pronouncing the dirty word "Israel." They used to call it the "Zionist entity," the "artificial creation," the "intrusion," the "infection," "Al Daula al-Maz'ouma"—the "artificial state," or the "artificial being." For a very long time many Arabs and most Palestinians maintained that Israel was some kind of mobile exhibition. If they protested loudly enough the world would take Israel and transplant it elsewhere, maybe to Australia or some other faraway place. They treated Israel like a nightmare, a *koshmar*; if they rubbed their eyes hard enough Israel would go away. They treated Israel like a passing infection; if they scratched it, it would go away somehow. And indeed they tried a couple of times, or actually several times, to undo Israel by military force. They failed and became very frustrated over this failure. But in the same years, the Israelis were no better. The Israelis, for their part, failed even to pronounce the explicit words "Palestinian people." We used to resort to euphemisms, such as the "locals" or the "Arab inhabitants of the land." We were more pan-Arabic than the Nasser regime in Egypt, because if you happen to be pan-Arabic, there is no Palestinian problem. The Arab world is huge. For many years we Israelis blinded ourselves to the fact that the Palestinian people could not find a home even in Arab countries. We did not want to see or hear this.

Those times are past. The two peoples now ought each to realize that the other is real; and most people on both sides now know that the other is not going to go away. Are they happy about it? Not at all. Is this a cheerful moment? Not at all. It's a painful moment. It's more like, for both sides, waking up in a hospital, after an anesthetized slumber and finding out that a limb has been amputated. And this, let me tell you, is a bad hospital and the doctors are not wonderful, and the two families outside the operating theater are cursing at each other and cursing the doctors. This is the picture of the Middle East right now. But everybody at least knows that surgery is unavoidable; everybody now knows that the country will have to be partitioned somehow into two national states. One country that will

be predominantly, not exclusively, but predominantly Jewish, because the Jews have a
right to be a majority in one small land, which,
after Israel's withdrawal, will probably be one-
third the size of a British county. But this will
be a place that will be recognized by Israeli
Jews, by the whole world, even by our neighbors, as our national home. But the price for
this must be that the Palestinian people will
have the same right. They will have a homeland, one that will be even smaller than Israel,
but will be home, their home.

More urgent, however, than the question of
boundaries, than the question of the disputed
holy places, more urgent than anything else,
is the question of what to do about the tragedy
of the Palestinian refugees of 1948. Those
people who lost their homes, and who in
some cases lost their homeland, lost everything during Israel's War of Independence in
1948. There is a deep disagreement on where

to put the blame, or most of the blame, for this tragedy. You will find some modern Israeli historians who put the blame on Israel. I suppose that in a few years, eventually, and I hope to live to see this day, you will find some modern Arab historians who put the blame on the Arab governments of that time. But regardless of who, finally, takes how much of the blame, this issue is urgent and immediate. Every Palestinian refugee who is homeless, and jobless, and countryless should be provided with a home and a job and a passport. Israel cannot admit these people, at least in vast numbers. If it does, it will no longer be Israel. Yet Israel should be part of the solution and should admit to part of the responsibility for this tragedy—though the degree of responsibility is a very academic and probably a very subjective question. But part of the responsibility lies with Israel. The other part lies with the Palestinian leadership of 1947 and with the

Arab governments of 1948. Israel has to help resettle the refugees in the future Palestine—that is, the West Bank and Gaza, or elsewhere. Of course, Israel is perfectly within its rights to bring up the subject of the one million Jewish refugees from Arab countries who lost their homes and their property following the 1948 war. These Jews don't want to go back to the Arab countries. But they, too, left everything behind—in Iraq, in Syria, in Yemen, Egypt, North Africa, in Iran and Lebanon—as they were literally pushed out of these countries, sometimes violently. So, all of this ought to be taken care of.

If I were prime minister of Israel, I would not sign any peace agreement that did not resolve the issues of the Palestinian refugees, by resettling them in the state of Palestine, because any resolution that doesn't take care of the issue of the refugees is a time bomb. Not only for moral reasons, but even for selfish reasons to do with Israel's security, this human and national problem must be resolved within the framework of the immediate peace process. Fortunately we are not speaking of the whole of Africa or India. We are talking about a few hundred thousand homes and jobs. Not every Palestinian refugee is homeless and country-less right now. But those who are, are rotting in inhumane conditions in refugee camps— their problem is my problem. If there is no solution for these people, Israel will have no peace and quiet even if it has an agreement with its neighbor.

I want to propose the first joint project that Israeli Jews and Palestinian Arabs will have to initiate once the divorce between them is conducted and the two-state solution is implemented. This project, for which we should take no foreign help, and for which the two nations should make an equal investment, dollar for dollar, ought to be a shared monument reflecting on our past stupidities, our past idiocies: To wit, everybody knows that when the peace treaty is finally implemented, the Palestinian people are going to get a lot less than they could have gotten fifty-five years ago, five wars ago, 150,000 dead ago, our dead and theirs. If only the Palestinian leadership in 1947–48 had been less fanatic and one-sided and less uncompromising, if only it had accepted the UN partition resolution of November 1947. But the Israeli leadership will also have to contribute to that monument to stupidity, because we Israelis could have gotten ourselves a much better deal, a much more convincing deal, if we had been less arrogant, less power-intoxicated, less selfish, and less unimaginative after out military victory in 1967.

So, the two nations will have a lot of soul searching to do, about their past mutual stupidities. However, the good news is that the

cognitive block is gone. If you passed a refer-
endum now, or a public-opinion survey between the Mediterranean and the River Jordan, asking every individual regardless of
religion, or status, or politics, or passport, or
lack of passport—every individual—not what
you would regard as a just solution, not what
you would like to see, but what you think is going to happen at the end of the day, I guess
about 80 percent would say: "a partition and a
two-state solution." Some would immediately
add: "And this will be the end of everything,
and a terrible injustice!" On both sides people
would say that. But, at least most of the people
know now. The good news is that, I think,
both the Jewish Israeli people and the Palestinian Arab people are ahead of their leaders,
for the first time in a hundred years. When finally a visionary leader stands up on both
sides and says: "This is it! This is it! Biblical
dreams—you may all go on dreaming them,

pre-'47 dreams, post-'67 dreams, these fantasies or those fantasies, you may go on dreaming, there is no censorship on fantasies. But the reality is roughly the 1967 lines." Give or take an inch here or there, by mutual agreement. And some open-ended formula for the disputed holy places, because only an open-ended arrangement can work there. In that moment, when the leaders on both sides are ready to say this, they will find the two peoples sadly ready for it. Not happy, but ready for it. More ready than ever before. Ready in the hard way, ready through pain and bloodshed, but ready.

I want to make one last point. What can you do? What can public-opinion-makers do? What can Europeans do? What can the outside world do, apart from shaking their heads and saying, "How terrible!"? Well, there are two things, perhaps three. One, public-opinion-makers across Europe are in the miserable habit of wagging their index finger, like an old-fashioned Victorian headmistress, at this side, or that side: "Aren't you ashamed of your-selves?" Too often I find in the papers of vari-ous European countries either terrible things about Israel or terrible things about the Arabs and about Islam. Simpleminded things, narrow-minded things, self-righteous things. I'm no longer a European in any sense, except through the pain of my parents and my ances-tors, who left forever in my genes a sense of unrequited love for Europe. But if I were a Eu-ropean, I'd be careful not to wag my finger at anyone at all. Instead of wagging your finger, calling the Israelis this name or the Palestini-ans that name, I would do anything I could to help both sides, because both are on the verge of making the most painful decision of their histories. The Israelis, by relinquishing the occupied territories, by removing most of the settlements, will have not only to retract their own self-image and face a serious internal clash and rift. They will be taking very serious security risks, not from Palestine, but from future extremist Arabic powers who may, one day, use Palestinian territory to launch an attack on Israel, which after the withdrawal will be only twelve kilometers wide at the hip. It means that the boundary of the future Palestinian state will start about seven kilometers from our one and only international airport. Palestine will be within twenty kilometers of about half the Israeli Jewish population. Jerusalem will be on the border. This is not an easy decision for the Israelis to make and yet they have to make it. The Palestinians, on their side, will have to sacrifice parts that were their own before 1948, and this is going to hurt. Good-bye Haifa, good-bye Jaffa, good-bye Beersheba, and many other towns and villages, which used to be Arabic and are no longer and will never again be part of Palestine. This is going to hurt like hell. So, if you have an ounce of sympathy to offer, now is the time to extend it to the two patients. You no longer have to choose between being pro-Israel and pro-Palestine. You have to be pro-peace.

how to cure a fanatic

how to cure a fanatic

So, how do you cure a fanatic? To chase a bunch of fanatics through the mountains of Afghanistan is one thing. To struggle against fanaticism is another one. I'm afraid I don't have any particular ideas on how to catch the fanatic in the mountains, but I do have one or two thoughts about the nature of fanaticism and the ways, if not to cure it, then at least to contain it. The attack on America on September 11 was not simply about poverty versus wealth. Poverty versus wealth is one of the world's most horrible problems, but we will misdiagnose such terrorist attacks if we simply think that this was an attack by the poor on the rich. It is not just about the "haves" and the "have-nots." If the case were as simple as that, you would rather expect the attack from Africa, the poorest, perhaps to be launched against Saudi Arabia and the Gulf, the oil-producing states, the richest. No, this is a battle between fanatics, who believe that the end, any end, justifies the means, and the rest of us, who believe that life is an end, not a means. It is a struggle between those who think that justice, whatever they would mean by the word, is more important than life, on the one hand, and those of us who think that life takes priority over many other values, convictions, or faiths. The present crisis in the world, in the Middle East, in Israel/Palestine, is not about the values of Islam. It is not about the mentality of the Arabs, as some racists claim, not at all. It is about the ancient struggle between fanaticism and pragmatism. Between fanaticism and pluralism. Between fanaticism and tolerance. September 11 was not even about the question of whether America was good or bad, whether capitalism is ugly, or whether globalization should stop or not. This was about the typical fanatic claim: If I think something is bad, I kill it along with its neighbors.

Fanaticism is older than Islam, older than Christianity, older than Judaism, older than any state or any government, or political system, older than any ideology or faith in the world. Fanaticism is unfortunately an ever-present component of human nature, an evil gene, if you like. People who blow up abortion clinics in America, people who burn mosques and synagogues in Europe, differ form bin Laden only in the scale but not in the nature of their crimes. Of course, September 11 evoked sadness, anger, disbelief, shock, melancholy, disorientation and, yes, some racist responses—anti-Arab and anti-Muslim racist responses—everywhere. Who would have thought that the twentieth century would be immediately followed by the eleventh century?

My own childhood in Jerusalem rendered me an expert in comparative fanaticism. Jerusalem of my childhood, back in the 1940s, was full of self-proclaimed prophets, redeemers, and messiahs. Even today, every other Jerusalemite has his or her personal formula for instant salvation. Everyone says they came to Jerusalem, and I'm quoting a famous line from an old song, they came to Jerusalem to build it and to be built by it. In fact, some of them—Jews, Christians and Muslims, socialists, anarchists, world reformers—actually came to Jerusalem not so much to build it, not so much to be built by it, but rather to get crucified, or to crucify others, or both. There is an established mental disorder, a recognized mental illness known as the "Jerusalem syndrome": People come to Jerusalem, they inhale the wonderful lucid mountain air, and then they suddenly get up and set fire to a mosque or a church or a synagogue. Or else, they simply take off their clothes, climb onto a rock and start prophesying. No one ever listens. Even today, even in today's Jerusalem, in every line waiting for a bus, conversation is likely to spark and turn into a fiery street seminar, with total strangers arguing about politics, morality, strategy, history, identity, religion, and the real purpose of God. Participants in such street seminars, while arguing about politics and theology, good and evil, try nevertheless to elbow their way to the front of the line. Everyone screams, no one ever listens. Except for me. I listen sometimes; that's how I earn my living.

Yet, I confess, as a child in Jerusalem, I was myself a brainwashed little fanatic all the way. Self-righteous, chauvinistic, deaf and blind to any view that differed from the powerful Jewish, Zionist narrative of the time. I was a stone-throwing kid, a Jewish Intifada kid. In fact, the first words I ever learned to say in English, except for "yes" and "no," were the words: "British, go home!" which was what we kids used to shout as we were throwing stones at the British patrols in Jerusalem. Talking about the ironies of history, in my 1995 novel, *Panther in the Basement*, I described how the boy, Proffy by name, or by nickname, loses his fanaticism, his chauvinism, up to a point at least, and is changed almost in the space of two weeks through a sense, a shade, of relativism. He happens to befriend, secretly, an enemy—a very sweet, ineffectual British police sergeant. And they meet secretly, the boy and the British sergeant, and they teach each other English and Hebrew. And the boy discovers that women have no horns and no tails, which is almost as shocking a revelation for this boy as the discovery that the British and Arabs have no horns and no tails. So, in a sense, the boy develops a sense of ambivalence, a capacity for abandoning his black-and-white views; but, of course, the price he pays is that by the end of this short novel he is no longer a child, he is a little grown-up, a small adult. Much of the joy and fascination and zeal and simpleness of life has gone away. And besides, he is getting a nickname, being called a traitor by his old friends. I am going to take the liberty of quoting from the first page and a half of *Panther in the Basement*,* because I think this is as close to myself, on the issue of fanaticism, as I could ever get.

> I have been called a traitor many times in my life. The first time was when I was twelve and a quarter and I lived in a neighbourhood at the edge of Jerusalem. It was during the summer holidays, less than a year before the British left the

* Translation by Nicholas de Lange (London: Vintage, 1997).

country and the state of Israel was born out of the midst of war.

One morning these words appeared on the wall of our house, painted in thick black letters, just under the kitchen window: PROFFY BOGED SHAFEL. "Proffy is a low-down traitor." The word *shafel*, "low-down," raised a question that still interests me now, as I sit and write this story. Is it possible for a traitor not to be low-down? If not, why did Chita Reznik (I recognize his writing) bother to add the word "low-down"? And if it is, under what circumstances is treachery not low-down?

I had had the nickname Proffy, attached to me every since I was so high. It was short for Professor, which they called me because of my obsession with checking words. (I still love words. I like collecting, arranging, shuffling, reversing, combining them. Rather the way people who love money so are the same with coins and banknotes and people who love cards do with cards.)

My father saw the writing under the kitchen window when he went out to get the newspaper at half past six that morning. Over breakfast, while he was spreading raspberry jam on a slice of black bread, he suddenly plunged the knife into the jam jar, almost up to the handle, and said in his deliberate way: "What a pleasant surprise. And what has His Lordship been up to now that we should deserve this honour?"

My mother said: "Don't get at him first thing in the morning, it's bad enough that he's always being got at by other children."

Father was dressed in khaki, like most men in our neighbourhood in those days. He had the gestures and voice of a man who is definitely in the right. Dredging up a sticky mass of raspberry from the bottom of the jar and spreading an equal amount on both halves of the slice of bread, he said:

"The fact is that almost everyone nowadays uses the word 'traitor' too freely. But what is a traitor? Yes indeed. A man without honour. A man who secretly, behind your back, for the sake of some questionable advantage, helps the enemy to work against his people. Or to harm his family and friends. He is more despicable than a murderer. Finish your egg, please. I read in the paper that people are dying of hunger in Asia."

Later on in this novel, the reader may find out that this characterization was totally wrong: Only he who loves might become a traitor. Treason is not the opposite of love; it is one of its many options. Traitor, I think, is the one who changes in the eyes of those who cannot change and would not change and hate change and cannot conceive of change, except that they always want to change you. In other words, traitor, in the eyes of the fanatic, is anyone who changes. And that's a tough choice, the choice between becoming a fanatic and becoming a traitor. In a sense, to not be a fanatic means to be, to some extent and in some way, a traitor in the eyes of the fanatic. I have made my choice, as *Panther in the Basement* will tell you.

I have called myself an expert on comparative fanaticism. This is no joke. If you ever hear of a school or university starting a department of comparative fanaticism, I am hereby applying for a teaching post. As a former Jerusalemite, as a recovered fanatic, I feel I'm fully qualified for that job. Perhaps it is time that every school, every university teach at least a couple of courses in comparative fanaticism, because it is everywhere. I don't mean just the obvious manifestations of fundamentalism and zealotry. I don't refer just to those obvious fanatics, the ones we see on television, in places where hysterical crowds wave their fists against the cameras while screaming slogans in languages we don't understand. No, fanaticism is almost everywhere, and its quieter, more civilized forms are present all around us and perhaps inside of us as well. Do I know the anti-smokers who will burn you alive for lighting a cigarette near them! Do I know the vegetarians who will eat you alive for eating meat! Do I know the pacifists, some of my colleagues in the Israeli peace movement, who are willing to shoot me right through the head just because I advocate a slightly different strategy on how to make peace with the Palestinians. I'm not saying, of course, that anyone who raises his or her voice against anything is a fanatic. I'm certainly not suggesting that anyone who has a strong opinion is a fanatic. I'm saying that the seed of fanaticism always lies in uncompromising self-righteousness, the plague of many centuries. Of course, there are degrees of evil. A militant environmentalist may be uncompromisingly self-righteous, but he or she will cause very little harm compared, say, to an ethnic cleanser or terrorist. Yet all fanatics have a special attraction, a special taste for kitsch. Very often the fanatic can only count up to one, two is too big a figure for him or her. At the same time, you will find that very often fanatics are hopelessly sentimental: They often prefer feeling to thinking and have a particular fascination with their own death. They despise this world and feel eager to trade it for "heaven." Their heaven, however, is usually conceived of as the everlasting happiness that occurs in the conclusion of bad movies.

Let me digress into a story; I'm a notorious

digresser, I always digress. A dear friend and colleague of mine, the wonderful Israeli novelist Sammy Michael, had once the experience that some of us writers have from time to time, of a very long intercity car drive with a chauffeur who was giving him the usual lecture on how urgent it is for us Jews to kill all the Arabs. And Sammy listened to him, and rather than screaming, "What a terrible man you are. Are you a Nazi, are you a fascist?" he decided to deal with it differently. He asked the chauffeur: "And who do you think should kill the Arabs?" The chauffeur said: "What do you mean? Us! The Israeli Jews! We must! There is no choice, just look at what they are doing to us every day!" "But who exactly do you think should carry out the job? The police? Or the army? Or maybe the fire brigade? Or the medical teams? Who should do the job?" The chauffeur scratched his head and said: "I think it should be fairly divided between every one of us, every one of us should kill some of them." Sammy Michael, still playing the game, said: "OK, suppose you are allocated a certain residential block of your hometown of Haifa and you knock on every door, or ring the doorbell asking: 'Excuse me, sir, or excuse me, madam, do you happen to be an Arab?' and if the answer is yes, you shoot them. Then you finish your block and you are about to go home, but just as you turn to go home," Sammy continued, "you hear somewhere on the fourth floor in your block a baby crying. Would you go back and shoot this baby? Yes or no?" There was a moment of quiet and then the chauffeur said to Sammy Michael: "You know, you are a very cruel man." Now, this is a significant story because there is something in the nature of the fanatic that essentially is very sentimental and at the same time lacks imagination. And this sometimes gives me hope, albeit a very limited hope, that injecting some imagination into people may help cause the fanatic to feel uneasy. This is not a quick remedy, this is not a quick cure, but it may help.

Conformity and uniformity, the urge to belong and the desire to make everyone else belong, may be the most widespread if not the most dangerous forms of fanaticism. Remember the moment in that wonderful film, Monty Python's *Life of Brian*, when Brian says to the crowd of his would-be disciples: "You are all individuals!" and the crowd shouts back: "We are individuals!" except one of them who says sheepishly, in a small voice: "I'm not," and everyone angrily rushes him. Indeed, having said that conformity and uniformity are mild but widespread forms of fanaticism, I have to add that very often the cult of personality, the idealization of political or religious leaders, the worship of glamorous individuals, may be another widespread form of fanaticism. The twentieth century seems to have excelled at both. Totalitarian regimes, deadly ideologies, aggressive chauvinism, violent forms of religious fundamentalism, on the one hand, and the universal idolization of a Madonna or a Maradona, on the other. Perhaps the worst aspect of globalization is the infantilization of humankind—"the global kindergarten" full of toys and gadgets, candies and lollipops. Up to the mid-nineteenth century, give or take a few years—it varies from one country to another, from one continent to another—but roughly, up to somewhere in the nineteenth century, most people in most parts of the world had at least three basic certainties: where I will spend my life, what I will do for a living, and what will happen to me after I die. Almost everyone in the world, just 150 or so years ago, knew that they were going to spend their lives right where they were born or somewhere nearby, perhaps in the next village. Everyone knew they would do for a living what their parents did for their living or something very similar. And everyone knew that, if they behaved themselves, they would be transformed to a better world after they died. The twentieth century has eroded, often destroyed, these and other certainties. The loss of these elemental certainties may have provided for the most heavily ideological half-century, followed by the most fiercely selfish, hedonistic, gadget-oriented half-century. For the ideological movements of the first half of the last century, the mantra was, "Tomorrow will be a better day—let's make sacrifices today; let's even impose sacrifices on other people today, so that our children will inherit a paradise in the future." Somewhere around the middle of that century, this was replaced by the notion of instant happiness, not just the famous right to strive for happiness, but the actual widespread illusion that happiness is displayed on the shelves and that all you have to do is make yourself rich enough to buy it with your wallet. The notion of "happily ever after," the illusion of lasting happiness, is actually an oxymoron. Either plateau or climax. Everlasting happiness is no happiness, just like an everlasting orgasm is no orgasm at all.

The essence of fanaticism lies in the desire to force other people to change. The common inclination to improve your neighbor, mend your spouse, engineer your child, or straighten up your brother, rather than let them be. The fanatic is a most unselfish creature. The fanatic is a great altruist. Often the fanatic is more interested in you than in himself. He wants to save your soul, he wants to redeem you, he wants to liberate you from sin, from error, from smoking, from your faith or from your faithlessness, he wants to improve your eating habits, or to cure you of your drinking or voting habits. The fanatic cares a great deal for you; he is always either falling on your neck because he truly loves you or else he is at your throat in case you prove to be unredeemable. And, in any case, topographically speaking, falling on your neck and being at your throat are almost the same gesture. One way or another, the fanatic is more interested in you than in himself, for the very simple reason that the fanatic has very little self or no self at all. Mr. bin Laden and his ilk do not just hate the West. It's not that simple. Rather, I think they want to save your souls; they want to liberate you, us, from our awful values, from materialism, from pluralism, from democracy, from freedom of speech, from women's liberation. . . . All these, the Islamic fundamentalists maintain, are very, very bad for your health. Bin Laden's immediate target may have been New York, or Madrid, but his goal was to turn moderate, pragmatic Muslims into "true" believers, into his kind of Muslim. Islam, in bin Laden's view was weakened by "American values," and to defend Islam, you must not just hit the West and hit it hard, you must eventually convert the West. Peace will prevail only when the world is converted not to Islam, but to the most fundamentalist and fierce and rigid form of Islam. It will be good for you. Bin Laden essentially loves you; by his way of thinking September 11 was a labor of love. He did it for your own good, he wants to change you, he wants to redeem you.

Very often, these things begin in the family. Fanaticism begins at home. It begins precisely with the very common urge to change a beloved relative for his or her own good. It begins with the urge to sacrifice oneself for the sake of a dearly loved neighbor; it begins with the urge to tell a child of yours, "You must become like me not like your mother," or "You must become like me not like your father," or "Please, become something very different from both your parents." Or, among married couples, "You have to change, you have to see things my way or else this marriage is not going to work." Very often it begins with the urge to live your life through someone else's life. To give yourself up in order to facilitate the next person's fulfillment or the next generation's well-being. Self-sacrifice very often involves inflicting dreadful feelings of guilt upon the beneficiary, thus manipulating, even controlling, him or her. If I had to choose between the two stereotypical mothers in the famous Jewish joke—the mother who says to her kid, "Finish your breakfast or I'll kill you," or the one who says, "Finish your breakfast or I'll kill myself"—I would probably choose the lesser of two evils. That is, rather not finish my breakfast and die, than not finish my breakfast and be guilt-ridden for the rest of my life.

Let us turn now to the gloomy role of fanatics and fanaticism in the conflict between Israel and Palestine, Israel and much of the Arab world. The Israeli-Palestinian clash is essentially not a civil war between two segments of the same population, or the same people, or the same culture. It is not an internal but an international conflict. Which is fortunate, as international conflicts are easier to resolve than internal ones—religious wars, class wars, value wars. I said easier, I did not say easy. Essentially the battle between Israeli Jews and Palestinian Arabs is not a religious war, although the fanatics on both sides are trying very hard to turn it into one. It is essentially no more than a territorial conflict over the painful question, "Whose land?" It is a painful conflict between right and right, between two very powerful, very convincing claims over the same small country. Not a religious war, not a war of cultures, not a disagreement between two traditions, but simply a real-estate dispute over whose house this is. And I believe that this can be resolved.

In a small way, in a cautious way, I do believe that imagination may serve as a partial and limited immunity to fanaticism. I believe that a person who can imagine what his or her ideas imply when it comes to the crying baby on the fourth floor, such a person may become a less complete fanatic, which is a slight improvement. I wish I could tell you at this point that literature is the answer because literature contains an antidote to fanaticism by injecting imagination into its readers. I wish I could simply prescribe: Read literature and you will be cured of your fanaticism. Unfortunately, it's not that simple. Unfortunately, many poems, many stories and dramas throughout history have been used to inflate hatred and nationalistic self-righteousness. Yet, there are certain works of literature that, I believe, can help up to a point. They cannot work miracles, but they can help. Shakespeare can help a great deal. Every extremism, every uncompromising crusade, every form of fanaticism in Shakespeare ends up either in a tragedy or in a comedy. The fanatic is never happier or more satisfied in the end; either he is dead or he becomes a joke. This is a good inoculation. And Gogol can help, too: Gogol makes his readers grotesquely aware of how little we know, even when we are convinced that we are 100 percent right. Gogol teaches us that your nose may become a terrible enemy, may even become a fanatic enemy, and you may find yourself fanatically chasing your own nose. Not a bad lesson in itself. Kafka is a good educator in this respect, although I am sure he never meant to be used as an education against fanaticism. Kafka shows us that there is darkness and enigma and mockery even when we think we have done nothing at all wrong. That helps. (And had we but world enough and time, I would go on at length about Kafka and Gogol and the connection, the subtle connection, I see between these two, but that's for another occasion.) And William Faulkner can help. The Israeli poet Yehuda Amichai expresses all of this better than I could ever hope to when he says "Where we are right no flowers can grow." It's a very useful line. So, to some extent, some works of literature can help, but not all of them.

And if you promise to take what I'm about to say with a big pinch of salt, I can tell you that, in principle at least, I think I have invented the remedy for fanaticism. A sense of humor is a great cure. I have never once in my life seen a fanatic with a sense of humor, nor have I ever seen a person with a sense of humor become a fanatic, unless he or she has lost that sense of humor. Fanatics are often sarcastic. Some of them have a very pointed sense of sarcasm, but no humor. Humor contains the ability to laugh at ourselves. Humor is relativism, humor is the ability to see yourself as others may see you, humor is the capacity to realize that no matter how righteous you are and how terribly wronged you have been, there is a certain side to life that is always a bit funny. The more right you are, the funnier you become. And, for that matter, you can be a self-righteous Israeli or a self-righteous Palestinian or a self-righteous anything, but as long as you have a sense of humor, you might be partially immune to fanaticism. If I could only compress a sense of humor into capsules and persuade entire populations to swallow my humor pills, thus immunizing everybody against fanatics, I might qualify one day for the Nobel Prize in medicine, not in literature. But just listen to me! The very idea of compressing a sense of humor into capsules, the very idea of making other people swallow my humor pills for their own good, thus curing them of their trouble, is already slightly contaminated with fanaticism. Be very careful, fanaticism is extremely catching, more contagious than any virus. You might easily contract fanaticism even as you are trying to defeat or combat it. You have only to read a newspaper, or watch the television news to see how easily people may become anti-fanatic fanatics, anti-fundamentalist zealots, anti-jihad crusaders. Eventually, if we cannot defeat fanaticism, perhaps we can at least contain it a little bit. As I have said, the ability to laugh at ourselves is a partial cure; the ability to see ourselves as others see us is another medicine. The ability to exist within open-ended situations, even to learn how to enjoy open-ended situations, to learn to enjoy diversity, may also help. I am not preaching a complete moral relativism, certainly not. I am trying to enhance our ability to imagine each other. On every level, on the most everyday level, to just imagine each other. Imagine each other when we quarrel, imagine each other when we complain, imagine each other precisely at the moment we feel that we are 100 percent right. Even when you are 100 percent right and the other is 100 percent wrong, it's still useful to imagine the other. In fact, we do it all the time. My last novel, *The Same Sea*, is about six or seven people who are scattered all over the globe and have between them an almost mystical communication. They sense each other, they communicate with each other all the time, in telepathic ways, although they are scattered in four corners of the earth.

The ability to exist within open-ended situations is, imaginatively, open to us all: Writing a novel, for instance, involves, among other burdens, the need to get up every morning, drink a cup of coffee, and start imagining the other. What if I were her, and what if you were him. And in my own personal background, in my own personal life story and family story, I can't help thinking, very often, that with a slight twist of my genes, or of my parents' circumstances, I could be him or her, I could be a Jewish West Bank settler, I could be an ultra-orthodox extremist, I could be an oriental Jew from a Third World country; I could be anyone. I could be one of my enemies. Imagining this is always a helpful practice. Many years ago, when I was still a child, my very wise grandmother explained to me in very simple words the difference between Jew and Christian— not between Jew and Muslim, but between Jew and Christian: "You see," she said, "Christians believe that the Messiah was here once and he will certainly return one day. The Jews maintain that Messiah is yet to come. Over this," said my grandmother, "over this, there has been so much anger, persecution, bloodshed, hatred. . . . Why?" she said. "Why can't everyone simply wait and see? If the Messiah comes, say-ing, 'Hello, it's nice to see you again,' the Jews will have to concede. If, on the other hand, the Messiah comes, saying, 'How do you do, it is very nice meeting you,' the entire Christian world will have to apologize to the Jews. Be-tween now and then," said my wise grand-mother, "just live and let live." She was defi-nitely immune to fanaticism. She knew the secret of living with open-ended situations, with unresolved conflicts, with the otherness of other people.

I began by saying that fanaticism often be-gins at home. Let me conclude by saying that the antidote can also be found at home, virtu-ally at your fingertips. No man is an island, said John Donne, but I humbly dare to add: No man and no woman is an island, but every-one of us is a peninsula, half attached to the mainland, half facing the ocean—one half connected to family and friends and culture and tradition and country and nation and sex and language and many other things, and the other half wanting to be left alone to face the ocean. I think we ought to be allowed to remain peninsulas. Every social and political system that turns each of us into a Donnean island and the rest of humankind into an enemy or a rival is a monster. But at the same time every social and political and ideological system that wants to turn each of us into no more than a molecule of the mainland is also a monstrosity. The condition of peninsula is the proper human condition. That's what we are and that's what we deserve to remain. So, in a sense, in every house, in every family, in every human condition, in every human connection, we actually have a relationship between a number of peninsulas, and we'd better remember this before we try to shape each other and turn each other around and make the next person turn our way while he or she actually needs to face the ocean for a while. And this is true of social groups and of cultures and of civilizations and of nations and, yes, of Israelis and Palestinians. Not one of them is an island and not one of them can completely merge with the other. These two peninsulas should be related and at the same time they should be left on their own. I know it is an unusual message in these days of violence and anger and revenge and fundamentalism and fanaticism and racism, all of which are loose in the Middle East and elsewhere. A sense of humor, the ability to imagine the other, the capacity to recognize the peninsular quality of every one of us may be at least a partial defense against the fanatic gene that we all contain.

the order of the teaspoon

an interview with amos oz,

september 2005[*]

BvR: The essays that form the basis of this book
were delivered as lectures in 2002. Much has
changed since then: Arafat's death, the new
Palestinian leader Abu Mazen, and, most recently, Sharon's pullout from Gaza. Do you
think that matters have been moving in a
positive direction?

Oz: I think Israel has taken a step in the right
direction by withdrawing the civilians and
army from Gaza. I would have done it differently. I would have done it as step one
in a comprehensive resettlement of the

---

[*] Interview was conducted over the telephone by Brigitta van
Rheinberg of Princeton University Press.

Palestinians. I would have tried to reach a comprehensive settlement on all the disputed issues and then implemented it gradually, beginning with Gaza. But even the way Sharon did it, it's a step in the right direction.

BvR: So it is a first step for solving what you have essentially called a "real estate conflict"?

Oz: It's a step, and let's take it in proportion. We have a long way to go, and, as the Arab proverb has it, "It is impossible to clap with one hand." Give it a try at my expense, and you will see that it is impossible. It will be necessary to see some Palestinian reciprocation in the area of taming their fanatics, at least making a start in taming the violence.

BvR: In that context, do you think that the chances for peace have improved with Abu Mazen's leadership?

Oz: What Abu Mazen is producing is a new language, and the new language is very important indeed. His language is much less violent and conflictual than the language of his predecessor. It is a secular language, it is a pragmatic language, and it is a peace-oriented language.

BvR: Do you think he will have the strength, ultimately, to impose that vision, and will the Palestinians follow him?

Oz: This is the big question, and I wish I had the answer. I am as eager as you are, and perhaps even more eager, to know the answer to that question: Does he actually have the strength, or, in other words, what is Palestinian public opinion? According to public opinion surveys in Palestine, week after week there is a majority of about 60 percent in favor of a pragmatic compromise with Israel. And you'll find the mirror image of that response on the Israeli side.

And, on both sides, week after week, public opinion polls also show that about 60 percent, plus or minus, are in favor of a two-state solution and a pragmatic compromise. I regard this as a huge improvement. When I started my activity with the Israeli Peace Movement advocating a two-state solution nearly forty years ago—Time flies! The Vietnam War was still raging!—the supporters of the two-state solution in Israel and in Palestine could conduct their national assembly inside the public telephone booths. This is a huge step forward.

BvR: So this is all really very encouraging, just looking at the numbers?

Oz: Yes, but even as we are encouraged, and encourage others, let us never underestimate the strength of the fanatics and their determination to derail any pragmatic compromise between Israel and Palestine. And I know that the fanatics on both sides are playing into each other's hands.

BvR: Speaking of fanatics and their potent ability to derail compromise, what do you think about the ongoing war in Iraq and the role it plays for the Israeli-Palestinian conflict?

Oz: If I understand correctly, the policy and the philosophy of the current American administration are not at all conservative. These people strike me as world reformers, not as conservatives. They want to install democracy in Iraq and perhaps all over the world, at gunpoint. This, I think, is unrealistic. It's not that I dismiss the gunpoints. I'm not a proponent of "Make love, not war." I've never been one. Vis-à-vis the Palestinians, my stance has always been, "Make peace, not love." After all, the opposite of war is not love: The opposite of war is peace. And yet, to install democracy, you need to encourage the growth and evolution of civil society. Without a civil society there can be no democracy. Civil society cannot evolve at gunpoint and it cannot evolve overnight. Nor can it evolve without some sort of a Marshall Plan. Despair and hopelessness are the greatest enemies of civil society and therefore of democracy.

BvR: It's interesting that you mention the Marshall Plan—do you see the Americans playing a similar role in the Middle East to the one they so successfully played in Europe after World War II?

Oz: I wish the present American administration, perhaps the present generation of Americans altogether, had more carefully studied their own history. I regard the Marshall Plan not only as the single most generous move in history, the single most generous policy in history, but also as the best investment anyone has ever made throughout history. It was the Marshall Plan that won the Cold War. Not ray guns and star wars, but the Marshall Plan. I think communism was defeated through the Marshall Plan, though its overthrow took thirty or forty years more to materialize. It was Harry Truman, not Ronald Reagan, who won the war through the Marshall Plan. But what was the essence of the Marshall Plan? It meant that America helped to reconstruct civil society—a ruined society—by preventing poverty and despair. I think something similar has to be implemented in the poorest parts of the world today. Not only by America: Europe must take part in it. Japan, which was previously on the receiving end of the equivalent of the Marshall Plan, should be one of the sponsors. In a small way, even Israel should symbolically take part.

BvR: Taking off from what you just said about the Marshall Plan and since the lectures were originally delivered to a European audience, is there anything you specifically want to communicate to an American audience?

Oz: Well, I just gave you my modest message. Reread your own history and reconsider the Marshall Plan. The war in Iraq and the war on terrorism and the war in Afghanistan are going to cost America almost as much as the Marshall Plan. Now I'm not suggesting that Americans should start to write checks. In the Middle East, writing checks will be encouraging corruption, and the checks will very soon end up in Swiss bank accounts. What is necessary is to work on the ground: for example, building homes for hundreds of thousands of Palestinian refugees who have been rotting in camps for almost sixty years. And I'm not now going into the less urgent question of who takes the blame for the suffering of the Palestinian refugees. The bottom line is that the blame be shared by Israel and the Arab world. But it is a luxury to discuss the division of blame. Helping the refugees is urgent, much more urgent than the issue of the disputed holy places. The refugees need 100,000 homes and maybe 200,000 jobs. These homes will have to be in the future state of Palestine, in the West Bank and Gaza, not inside Israel; otherwise, there will be two Palestinian states and not even one for the Israelis. Such a project is not rebuilding the entire Third World; this is not all of Africa. This is more or less the equivalent of the effort the United States will have to invest in the state of Louisiana. This is, I think, a burning, key issue. So here is my message, and this is to

Americans as much as it is to Europeans: Rather than the finger wagging, whether this finger wagging is aimed at Israel (Be ashamed of yourselves! How can you be such shameless oppressors of the Palestinians!), or at the Arabs and the Palestinians (Aren't you ashamed to be such bloody terrorists!), this Victorian headmistress style isn't working. What we need on both sides is practical help. Let me give you a simple example: all those annoying and oppressive Israeli roadblocks in the occupied territory. Much of this could have been resolved if the rich countries had pooled their resources and helped build a tunnel—thirty miles, less than thirty miles—between Gaza and the West Bank. There would be no roadblocks, and the issue of Palestinian territorial cohesion could be resolved by a four-lane highway and a railway between Gaza and the West Bank underneath Israeli territory. We're not even talking billions; we're talking reasonable sums of money. This would have helped to resolve the problem. The finger wagging is a waste of time, and it creates resentment, among both Israelis and Palestinians.

BvR: As one of Israel's best-known writers and most outspoken public intellectuals, and as somebody who has been involved in two of your country's wars but also played a role in the Israeli Peace Movement, how do you see your own role?

Oz: I regard myself as a modest country doctor. This is a very different tradition, you know. Both in Europe and in the American tradition when you see an injustice, you launch an angry demonstration against the bad guys, sign an enthusiastic petition empathizing with the good guys, and you go to sleep feeling good. I come from a

very different tradition. When I see people
bleeding in the roads, the last thing that
matters to me at that instant is who caused
the accident. I ask myself, what can I actually do as an individual? If I have some
medical training, I will tend injuries. If I
don't, I will bring water. I make a phone
call; I try to comprehend. This is what my
colleagues and I in the Israeli Peace Movement have been doing for thirty-five years,
and this is what our Palestinian colleagues
in the Palestinian Peace Movement have
been doing. Rather than just signing petitions (and we do sign petitions), rather than
just launching demonstrations (and we do
launch demonstrations from time to time),
what we essentially try to do is create person-
to-person contact. We try to sit and discuss
and make practical proposals for every disputed issue. Now the leaders are not quite
ready for the proposals brought forth by

the peace movements in Israel and Palestine, but we have prepared an effective prescription for every one of these issues—refugees, settlements, holy places, boundaries, security, economy. We are trying to educate people and persuade them to swallow this bitter medicine they don't like; it's not a pleasant medicine.

BvR: In the book, you describe yourself as "a brainwashed little fanatic," growing up in Jerusalem. Do you think that this polarizing climate you describe and experienced in your youth has changed on both sides?

Oz: There are different sets of clocks that work simultaneously. On one hand, there is more pragmatism on both sides now, not as a result of our work but as a result of the harsh slap of reality. Both sides have learned a bitter lesson by battering each other. They are both bleeding, and they have been bleeding for decades. At the same time, fanatics never tire, and fanaticism is on the rise not only in the Middle East but all over the world. There is a rise of Islamic fanaticism, there is a rise of Jewish fanaticism, and indeed there is a rise of Christian fanaticism, or fundamentalism. To me there is no difference between people who blow up abortion clinics in America and people who blow up the World Trade Center towers, except in the scale of their actions. The principle is the same. So we must be vigilant, because fanaticism is gathering strength even as many individuals are seeking pragmatic compromise. Fanatics are getting more enthusiastic, and more eager to derail compromise.

BvR: You've said that you don't see the conflict as civilizational, religious, cultural; you see it as an ancient struggle about fanaticism and tolerance, and an ever-present component of human nature—an evil gene, if you like. Is there anything unique to the conflict, in your mind?

Oz: I think I express it in the essay on fanatics: This is a conflict between two former victims of the same oppressor. That makes it not easier but harder. As we may know from individual experience, from family experience—some of the worst conflicts are precisely those between two victims of the same oppressor, two children of the same violent parent. They look at each other and see the image of the violent parent. Now this is very much the case between the Israelis and the Palestinians, and between Israelis and Arabs. And let us not forget that both Jews and Arabs have been defeated, humiliated, discriminated against, and widely persecuted and oppressed by European civilization. Let us never forget it. Americans may feel that they have nothing to do with this

European/Middle East complexity of relations, and yet they should be aware of that history.

BvR: What role does the history of the Jews play in your mind, considering that it has often been described as a history of suffering and victimhood?

Oz: The role in my mind is not so much the fact that the Jews were victims—the Jews were not the only oppressed people in history as you know. Rather, the conflict is one between two victims. Both sides have internalized the self-image of a victim, which often begets a certain degree of self-righteousness, neurosis, and insecurity. This I find among both Jews and Arabs. In this respect Jews and Arabs are tragically similar—insecurity, self-righteousness, a sense of everlasting victimhood. You know, even when the problem of Israel and Palestine is resolved, and Israel and Palestine agree to exchange ambassadors and establish diplomatic relations, even when this conflict is history, there will still be bitter disagreement about who was the victim and who the tormentor. And neither of the parties will ever give up its claim to victimhood. It's part of the human comedy, and we can live with it. After all, we don't have to agree about the past; we only have to agree about the present and the future.

BvR: Some of the remedies you prescribe in the book are a good sense of humor, reading Shakespeare and Kafka, learning how to imagine the other. I couldn't help but wonder whether some people might not consider this utterly unrealistic and a hopelessly idealistic way of looking at the world.

Oz: The country doctor that I am prescribes imagining the other, and a sense of humor. Not as a substitute for realistic compromise, but as a necessary preparation. We need a

compromise; we need a contract; we need a
real-estate solution; we need to divide the
house into apartments, into a duplex. Good-
will and a sense of humor are no substitute
for this, but they will provide the right at-
mosphere. Now I think this goes beyond
the conflict in the Middle East. Imagining
the other, in my view, is not only an aes-
thetic business. It's an ethical imperative.
Inside the family—not just between nations
or between communities—imagining the
other is a moral imperative. I want to tell
you a secret (don't quote me): I think that
imagining the other is also a great pleasure.
A secret pleasure and a great pleasure. I
think imagining the other turns us not only
into better neighbors, or better spouses; it
even turns us into better lovers.

BvR: And in so many ways, imagining the
other is of course also what literature is all
about.

Oz: This is exactly the link between my literary work and my political work. I have never been in the business of good guys and bad guys. I know some conflicts are between good and evil, but they are of less interest to me in literature and in life. I am always, country doctor that I am, fascinated by the conflict between right and right, by the complex, not the simple, conflicts. In the twentieth century, many of the conflicts were very simple. Fascism, Nazism, and anti-fascism: Every decent human being knew where to stand, even if you woke him in the middle of the night. Colonialism, de-colonialization, apartheid, the war in Viet-nam: If you were a decent human being you knew where you stood. The conflict in the Middle East is not one of these. It's a painful and tragic clash between right and right and sometimes between wrong and wrong—very often between wrong and wrong. But that is precisely why this conflict fascinates me, and it also fascinates me in my literary work. I never write about good guys and bad guys; I write about clashes within families, between people who are both right, or both partly right.

BvR: So let me put a final question to you, very broad and general: Is there hope of curing the fanatics one day?

Oz: Once, I claimed that all this was a bad dream, but it is going to stay with us. This is not something that's going to vanish from the face of the earth, but we can contain it. Not completely cure it, but contain it. And when I speak about humor as a cure for fanaticism, take my prescription with a grain of salt. I suggest that everyone take it with a grain of salt: If you don't, you don't have a sense of humor. Yes, I think that humor is a great healer, but how to instill humor in people, how to make people capable of laughing at themselves, in other words, how to make them see themselves the way other people see them—well, in the very long run, reading novels is a big help, but not a magic cure. There are not a lot of magic formulas for anything. I am not a radical, although I have the reputation of being a raving radical in some circles in my country. But I have never been one. I am an evolutionist. My life, private and public, has taught me to be very patient with medicine. You are dealing with a disease, and with a patient with many relatives. And sometimes the patient is stupid or refuses to follow your prescription. The country doctor that I am keeps saying, try again, try one more time.

Let us conclude with my story of the Order of the Teaspoon. I believe that if one person is watching a huge calamity—let's say a conflagration—there are always three principal options. Option 1: Run away, as far away and as fast as you can, and let those who cannot run burn. Option 2: Write a very angry letter to the editor of your paper demanding that the responsible people be removed from office in disgrace. Or for that matter, launch a demonstration. Option 3: Bring a bucket of water and throw it on the fire, and if you don't have a bucket, bring a glass, and if you don't have a glass, use a teaspoon—everyone has a teaspoon. And yes, I know a teaspoon is little and the fire is huge, but there are millions of us and each one of us has a teaspoon. Now I would like to establish the Order of the Teaspoon. People who share my attitude—not the run-away attitude, or the letter attitude, but the tea-spoon attitude—I would like them to walk around wearing a little teaspoon on the lapel of their jackets, so that we know that we are in the same movement, in the same brotherhood, in the same order, the Order of the Teaspoon. This is my philosophy in a nutshell—or in a teaspoon, if you wish.